Passive Income

More Money Everyday Without Working A Job

Chandra Dhopatkar

Indirect Knowledge Limited

Jackson, Michigan

Indirect Knowledge Publishing
4023 Briggs Ct.
Jackson, MI/49201
www.indirectknowledge.com

Publisher's Note: Although the publisher and the author have made every effort to ensure that the information in this book was correct at press time and while this publication is designed to provide accurate information in regard to the subject matter covered, the publisher and the author assume no responsibility for errors, inaccuracies, omissions, or any other inconsistencies herein and hereby disclaim any liability to any party for any loss, damage, or disruption caused by errors or omissions, whether such errors or omissions result from negligence, accident, or any other cause.

This publication is meant as a source of valuable information for the reader, however it is not meant as a substitute for direct expert assistance. If such level of assistance is required, the services of a competent professional should be sought.

Passive Income/ Chandra Dhopatkar. -- 1st ed.
ISBN 9798702011738

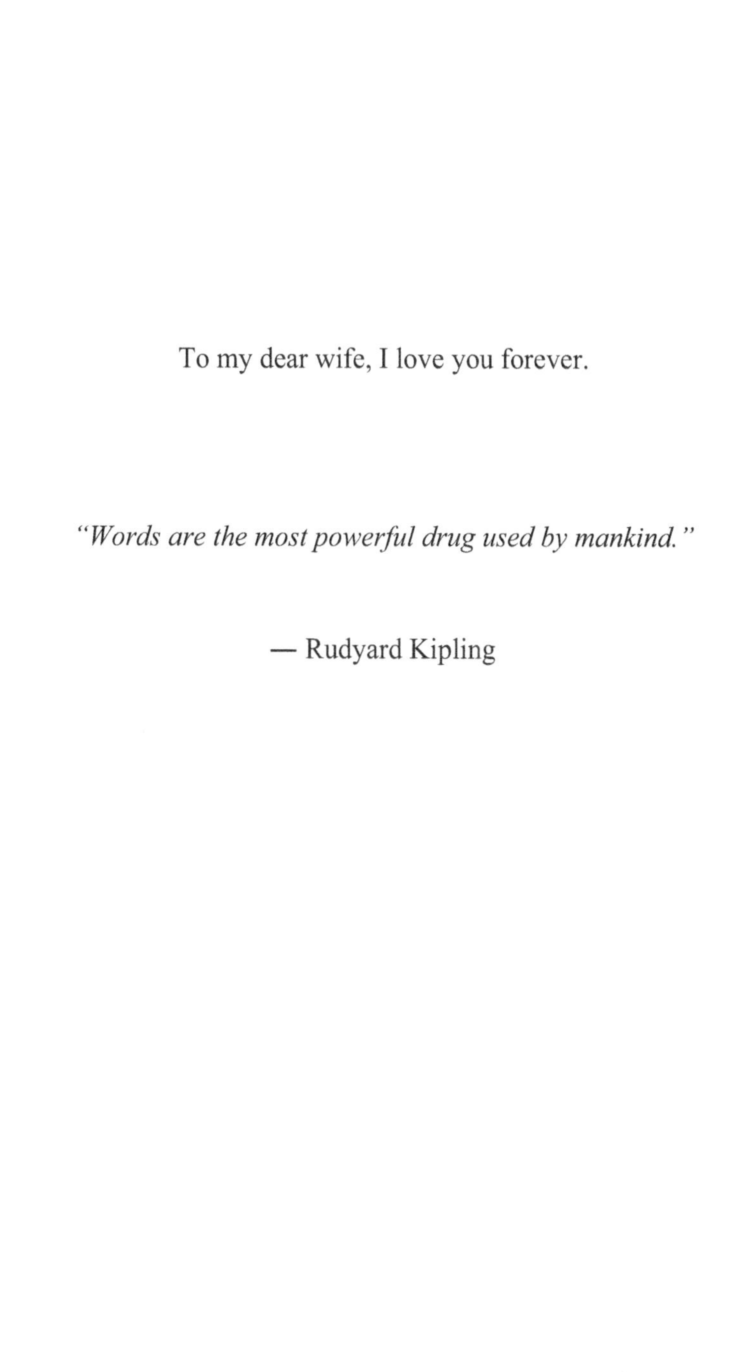

To my dear wife, I love you forever.

"Words are the most powerful drug used by mankind."

— Rudyard Kipling

CONTENTS

CHAPTER 1

The Best Ways to Create Passive Income

Passive income is income that takes little to no work to bring in and keep. It's also known as progressive income since the passive earner only expends little effort on his or her income to increase the income. Examples of passive income come from any activity where the person doesn't physically participate and earns the income passively. This can include stocks and bonds, interest, rental income, and a variety of other things. The passive earner usually receives a check instead of an hourly wage.

If you're looking for a passive income strategy, start by saving some money to invest in the stock market. Many experts advise against investing in the stock market since the real value of stocks has declined dramatically over time, so it's always best to invest in mutual funds or a savings account. If you do want to invest in the stock market, then you should do so with your children's help. Have them invest in mutual funds with you. Don't use your children's savings account to invest because if the market takes a bad turn, it could hurt their accounts.

Another option for passive income is to invest in dividend paying stocks. Most of the time, companies issue a dividend each year, which represents their share of profits from the equity holders. These companies pay a dividend because it's a tax-deductible expense. For most stocks, this isn't a very risky strategy because the returns are normally good over time. Dividends are paid quarterly and you have to wait until the following quarterly date to receive your payment.

Another passive income strategy involves real estate investment. Properties are bought and then resold, earning an income from the rental properties that are developed. You don't have to do any of the work like buying and selling, although it can be helpful. The properties generally increase in value and you can earn a good return on your investment.

Passive income is also created through the accumulation and buildup of residual income. Residual income means your salary as well as other regular expenses, such as housing, utility bills, and insurance. Residuals are most often earned through corporate finance and professional services. Corporate finance refers to the strategies and tools used by corporations to acquire, manage, and utilize capital to maximize shareholder wealth.

There are various ways you can generate passive income through investments. Some methods are more risky than others. You could invest in the stock market, but you may not get the best return on your investment unless you have years of experience in the business. Another option for passive income streams is to invest in rental properties. To rent out property, you must advertise and manage the property yourself.

If you want to create passive income streams, another option is a real estate investment. You need to determine the amount of rental income you plan to generate and invest in a piece of property. Real estate investing is popular among retirees who want to supplement their income. You could purchase rental properties, wait for the tenants to pay you, and then do your own maintenance and repairs. When you decide to sell the property, you will earn a tidy profit.

Commercial properties come in a wide range of prices. You can invest in apartment buildings, office buildings, condos, or retail stores. These businesses are much more stable than apartment buildings. You can also opt for a partnership business with other retirement-age people. A number of seniors have decided to invest in commercial properties together, creating an income-generation network. You can also opt for the stock market to invest in stocks and bonds, though this method is less predictable than passive income-generation methods.

CHAPTER 2

Building an Online Passive Income Business Using 9 Steps to Build a New Income Stream

As you know, the internet is growing at an alarming rate. The reason why is because people are constantly looking for new ways to make money online. Many have found their niche and want to know how they can create online passive income. The good news is that creating passive sources of residual income is much easier than you think. You don't even have to know much of anything about computers. Here's how you can create a steady stream of residual income:

Step One: Find your niche. If you do not know what your niche is right now, do a quick search. If you only know what you like to do, look for opportunities to make money online by providing affiliate links on your blog site. Once you have come up with several ideas, you should take action on them immediately.

Step Two: Build your products. If you do not know how to build your online passive income online, there are many opportunities to learn from the gurus on the internet. Once you have a few products in your possession, start promoting them on different websites. You can also sit back and watch the traffic roll in.

Step Three: Generate revenue. Once you have plenty of products, the next step is to create an affiliate program. In other words, you create a program where you will recruit a member for every person that they send to your site using your affiliate link. This is another way to generate a passive income stream. It is a lot easier than writing new posts for your blog or sending out e-mails to your list of subscribers.

Step Four: Distribute your digital products. Once you have a few members, it is time to get your hands dirty and distribute your digital products. For example, you could create an online course. In addition to offering the course through your affiliate links, you could also offer it for free as an eBook download. The last thing you want to do is send a bunch of affiliate links across the web; that would be a very bad idea.

Step Five: Make easy digital downloads. Once your digital products have been distributed and you have earned some passive income, the time comes to build an e-book and get it out there for sale. Again, don't send out e-mail solicitations to everyone on your list. The best thing to do is offer an e-book for download for $2.99 or less.

Step Six: Setup a website with a sales sign in. This is the final step to setting up an online passive income system. You will need to promote the site; you can do this by adding a WordPress plug-in to your blog. A WordPress affiliate plugin will make it very easy to display sales ads, track subscribers and even build an email campaign and subscriber list.

Step Seven: Build a whole notion around your affiliate products. Your new post will provide insight or new content about your affiliate product and encourage people to purchase them. That's basically it! When people read your new posts, they are going to buy something, and that something is your affiliate products.

Step Eight: Create a whole new online course. Now that your passive income site has shown people what you can do, it is time to launch a new book or mini-course. Offer it as a new blog post, a free download, a giveaway item, a newsletter sign-up, and whatever other promotional method you like. You can promote your whole new course through your affiliate links and earn money from your new readers and subscribers.

Step Nine: Invest in yourself. The first part of this nine-step process is simple enough: you need to invest in your future by taking small and consistent financial steps. Get more education, invest in yourself, start a business that you know you'll be passionate about for the long haul. Start seeing the world the way others see it, and being willing to make changes to it if need be. This second part of the process is almost as important as the first, so don't skip over it.

Step Ten: Find a good passive income lending club. Now that you have an established readership and a new course, it is time to consider investing in your future. Look into investing in a residual income or affiliate lending club. A lending club is just what it sounds like: a group that invests in people who are already successful. These clubs typically give people a patreon share or commission for each sale they make. So if you make a sale a couple of times per month, you will be given a commission.

CHAPTER 3

How to Make Passive Income From a Passive Income Stream

Passive income comes from an external source other than a regular employer or employee. Many of us believe that passive income refers to receiving something for free, but in actuality, it still involves effort on your part. Essentially, you're giving the work for free. This type of income isn't quite as common as other forms of income, but it can be very lucrative and is definitely worth considering if you have the time, desire, and resources to devote to making it a success.

The best example of this particular type of passive income is through social media. If you've ever used Twitter or another microblogging site to make money, then you have some experience with the concept. With social media, you essentially act as a middleman for the social media company, which pays you for the advertising space on your blog or website so you can make money from the company.

As an example, consider Twitter, a great microblogging site where millions of people can communicate at the same time. Each time someone comments on your blog or site, you get paid. The payouts can be in the form of a percentage of sales (such as a percentage of book sales) or in the form of a flat monetary royalty. With these types of royalty payments, you make money only if you actually sell a physical product or service. However, by using a service like Direct Deposit, you can receive your royalties in real time via electronic funds transfer, further boosting your earning potential as an affiliate marketer.

Another example of passive income comes in the form of affiliate marketing. This type of income allows you to promote someone else's products or services on your own site and earn a commission each time a sale or lead is generated. In order to take full advantage of this opportunity, it is important that you understand the intricacies of affiliate marketing and how it works. It is also vital to learn the different ways to earn commissions through the use of social media. In particular, you must master the art of email marketing, content marketing, and social media in order to optimize your passive income potential.

Many people who are trying to use their passive income to build an Internet empire tend to over complicate things. Instead, they should take a step back and simplify things. Here are some examples:

There are many ways to monetize your passive income. One great way is to hire a ghostwriter to write articles that contain links to your own products and services. By hiring a ghostwriter, you can focus on promoting your own products while he writes articles about them. Ghostwriters are also a great way to create original content for your site.

Another good way to make money from a passive income stream is to use Google's AdSense program. All you have to do is put a few code words into your website's HTML code and you'll be given ads that you can place on your site. The more targeted traffic you drive to your site, the better chance you have of earning some passive income from AdSense. The key to making money with AdSense is attracting quality traffic; if you want to learn how to make money with Google AdSense, all you have to do is research a bit and find out what AdSense keywords are most popular with advertisers.

If you really want to capitalize on your passive income stream, consider selling your own e-book. The best way to sell your first book is to co-write one yourself. You can create a whole new market for yourself by creating a self-publishing blueprint that consists of everything you need to know to make a great profit from selling your own e-books. This blueprint will show you how to choose an area of personal finance, invest your money, and even how to start your own e-book publishing company so that you can start earning money right away. Once you have a successful self-publishing business, then you can branch out and sell other products.

Earn Residual Income by Setting Up Affiliate Marketing Programs

Many people are asking if there is any such thing as residual income, and the answer is yes. Residual income is earned in a host of different ways ranging from regular stock dividends to music royalties. A lot of people seem to confuse the term with residual income, but the two are actually very different. Here's what you need to know.

Jeffshavitz explained that residual income is simply earning money over time, instead of making it all at once. He said that this could be done through "making money at one job in your 30s, then working at another job for a couple of years, and then doing it all again." Essentially, you're putting in your 30 years of service at one company and then transitioning into another company. The trick is to make sure you continue to make money for a minimum of six months to a year, before transitioning to the next opportunity.

The trick is the hard work. Jeffshavitz makes it sound so easy, but people often overlook the hard work that is required. It doesn't take a genius to understand that there is a lot of hard work behind making money with residual income. You've got to get out there, find prospects, and train them properly. It takes a lot of creativity to come up with new marketing ideas and campaigns to promote your products and/or services. It also takes a lot of hard work to follow through with the training.

So, what can you do to create residual income with eBook writing and publishing? One option is to use affiliate programs. You can set up an affiliate account and offer to write books for others. This will require you to invest some money upfront, but if you're smart, the cost will be recouped in commissions. You'll also earn commissions on any sales that result from customers buying products because of your recommendations.

Another option is to become a ghostwriter. This can take some time to get going, but once you get it going, it can bring in residual income for years to come. A good way to break into this field is to pick an ebook and ghostwrite it. Once published, you can then publish another book as a client's ghostwriter. If you produce quality books, you can command a high price and make a lot of money.

If you prefer to self-publish your own eBook instead of publishing through an affiliate program or through a ghostwriting service, you can still earn residual income by selling your own books. All you need to do is promote your ebooks by submitting them to various sites and participating in forums on the Internet. You can even join discussion groups and blog in the Internet to build your reputation.

One of the best ways to create residual income with your writing career is to invest in stock market investing. There are many websites that allow you to invest in stocks. You can buy and sell books that discuss the investing techniques and you will be able to earn residual income from the profits you make from investing. To become a stock market investor, all you have to do is purchase a stock at a price that you deem low. Once you turn a profit, you can sell the stock at a higher price and earn more money. You can also hold on to the stock for several months and wait for it's value to go up again before selling it.

If you want to do something interesting and fast, you can try a two-for-one wahm business. This wahm is a great opportunity for you to not only earn residual income, but to also make money while you are learning how to make an internet business for yourself. Basically, you have two opportunities: one where you get a percentage of the sale (the affiliate commission) and another where you sell a product and receive a fixed amount from the sale of that product. Two for one who is a very powerful combination because it will allow you to not only make good money on the affiliate commissions you earn, but also allow you to earn residual income that continues to come in even after you stop making sales.

CHAPTER 5

Passive Income Ideas - Where Can I Earn Income With Passive Income?

Passive income is income that you earn from a method that takes very little to no effort to keep up. In order to achieve a passive income, you'll need to find a method that can be set up over time so that your profits increase without you having to constantly do what it takes to promote the business. Some passive income ideas such as building a blog or renting out a property can take quite a bit of work to get started, but once you get it going, you can earn money even while you're sleeping. There are many different ways to make passive income, and one of the most popular is through affiliate marketing. You will need to learn a few things before getting started though, and here are some ways to make passive income using affiliate marketing:

Create several retirement plan account savings. Invest the money in a variety of high-risk, high reward investments, such as stocks, bonds, real estate and bonds. When you're planning for your retirement, be sure to take this factor into consideration. There are many different ways to create multiple passive income streams with retirement accounts. You can take the money you make from your investment returns and invest them in additional investments, build a foundation for a retirement plan, or save for a future earning.

Rent out your rental property. There are two major ways to make passive income from your rental property, through rent payments or by allowing a property management company to do the repairs and maintenance on your rental property. If you focus on the first option, making passive income from rent payments, then you'll have more income to put toward retirement. The same holds true if you focus on the second option, having a property management company do all the upkeep and repairs on your rental properties. You'll make more money from your rental properties, but you won't have to worry about paying a large amount out-of-pocket for the repairs, maintenance and so forth.

Build a retirement plan. Your retirement plan should be one that takes care of your entire life, and not just your retirement. As with any investment, your goal with your retirement plan should be to build passive income, so you can live on your investment gains and still have money available to spend on living expenses, and your family once you stop working.

Use the stock market to make passive income. One of the best passive income options to earn an income from is to invest in the stock market. You don't have to hold shares or invest in individual companies. Instead, you can invest in the market and make small initial investments to see if the company goes up in value over time. If it does, you can make money by buying and selling the stock at a profit.

Earn money with auctions. Many people are familiar with the idea of having an auction in your home to raffle off things you own and no longer need. There are many websites that offer this as one of many passive income options. Others involve going to raffle sales in stores where there is merchandise you can bid on, such as CDs, jewelry, China or antiques. The idea is that you win and then keep the item, or in some cases, sell it later to make money.

Rent out space in your house. These passive income options include renting out an extra room in your home to someone who is interested in doing business with you, but may not have a product of their own to sell. You can also find websites that will let you rent out unused rooms in your home and they will pay you per day, week or month for the use of the room. This is another excellent passive income option.

Passive income is more easily obtained than most people believe. When you have one or more of these income options, consider what you can do to maximize them and how much they can help you in your daily life. The possibilities are endless with passive income!

ABOUT THE AUTHOR

Chandra Dhopatkar is a content writer who formerly worked as an internet marketer. A content writer by day and a home chef by night, he is loath to discuss himself in the third person but can be persuaded to do so from time to time.

Learn more about him:

www.indirectknowledge.com